Calming Mandalas
Easy Coloring Book

Vol.7

Viola Halls

DEDICATION

For all who need relaxation and keeping calm.

Mandala 1

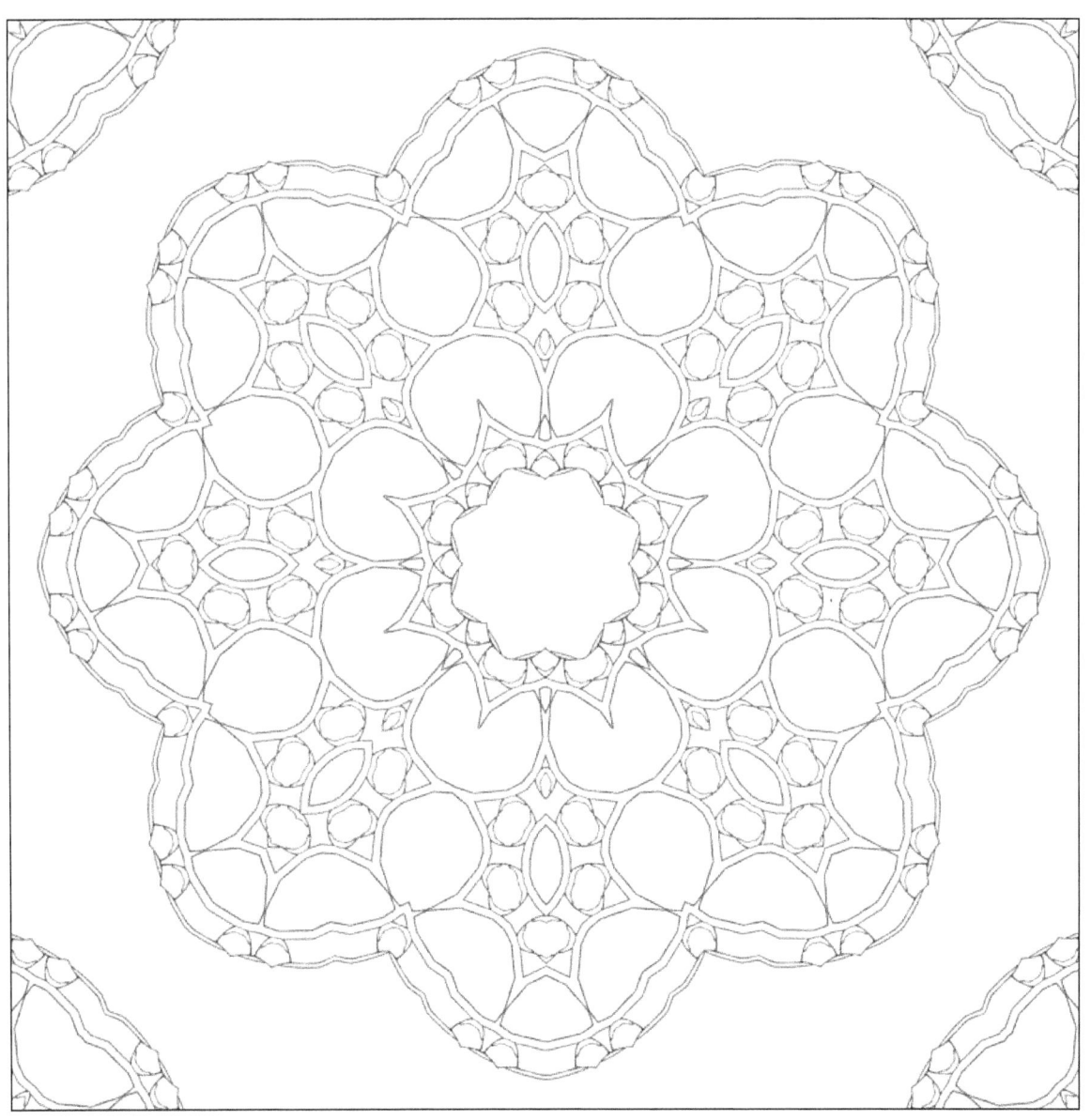

Mandala 2

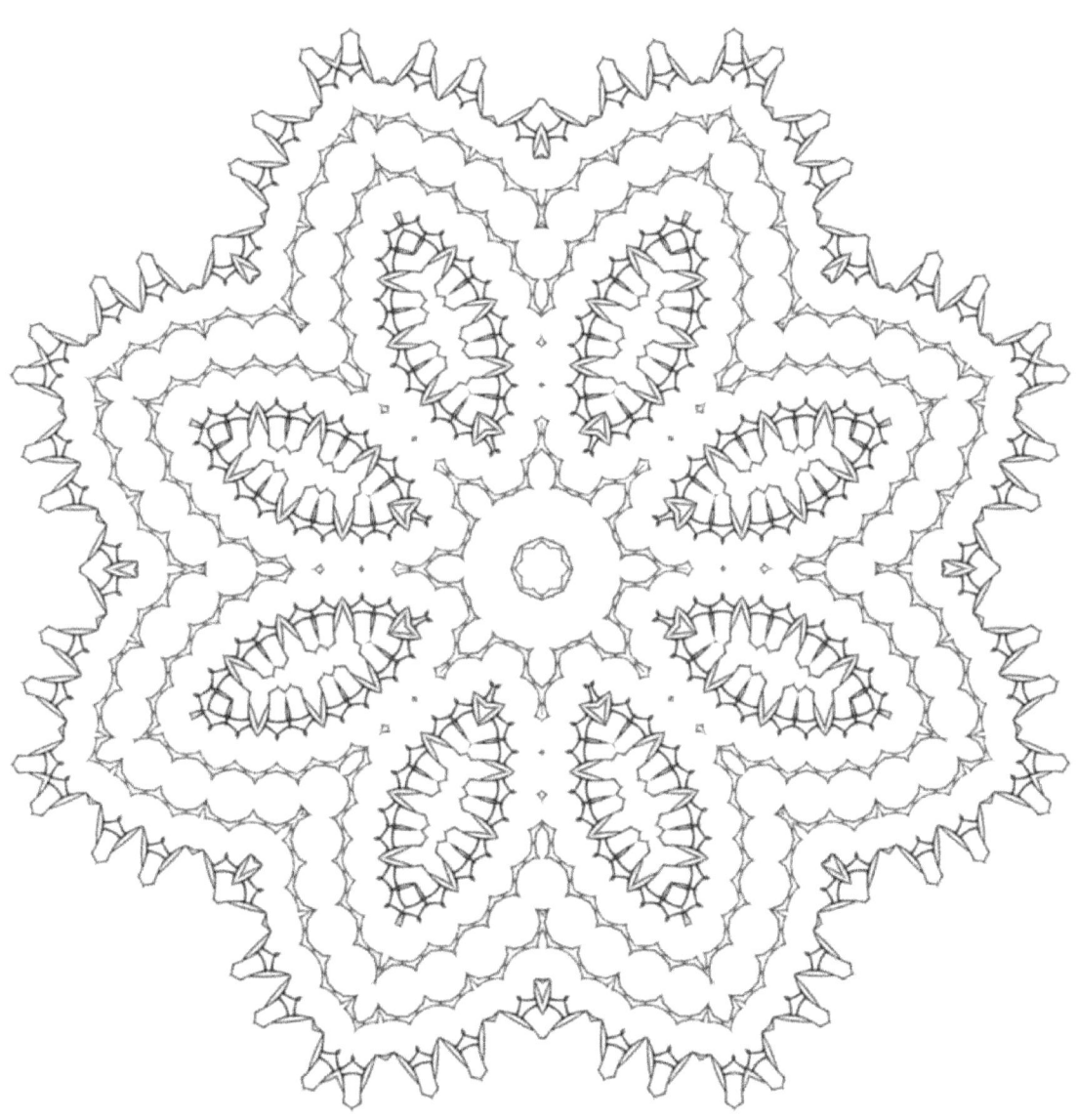

Mandala 3

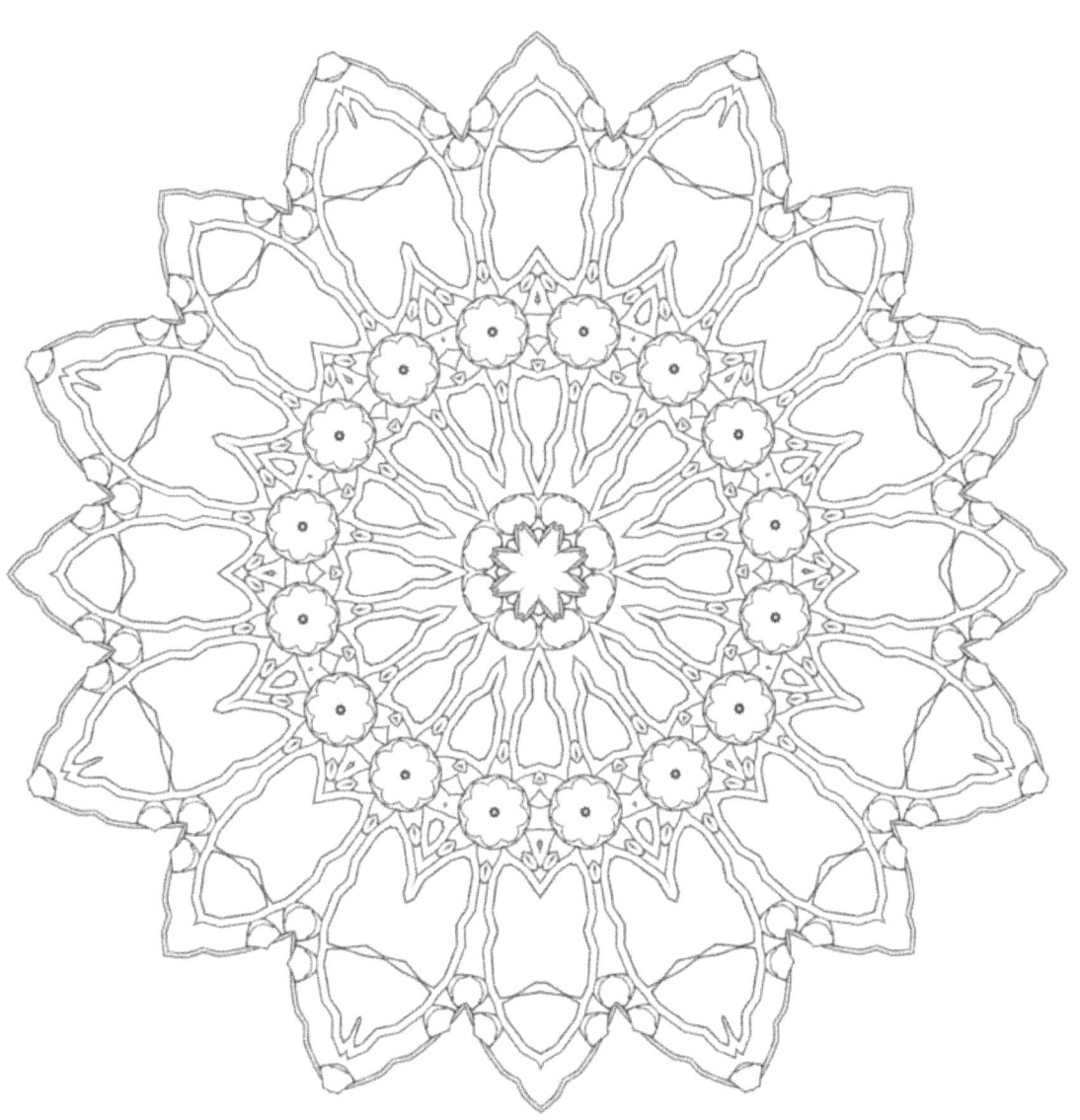

Mandala 4

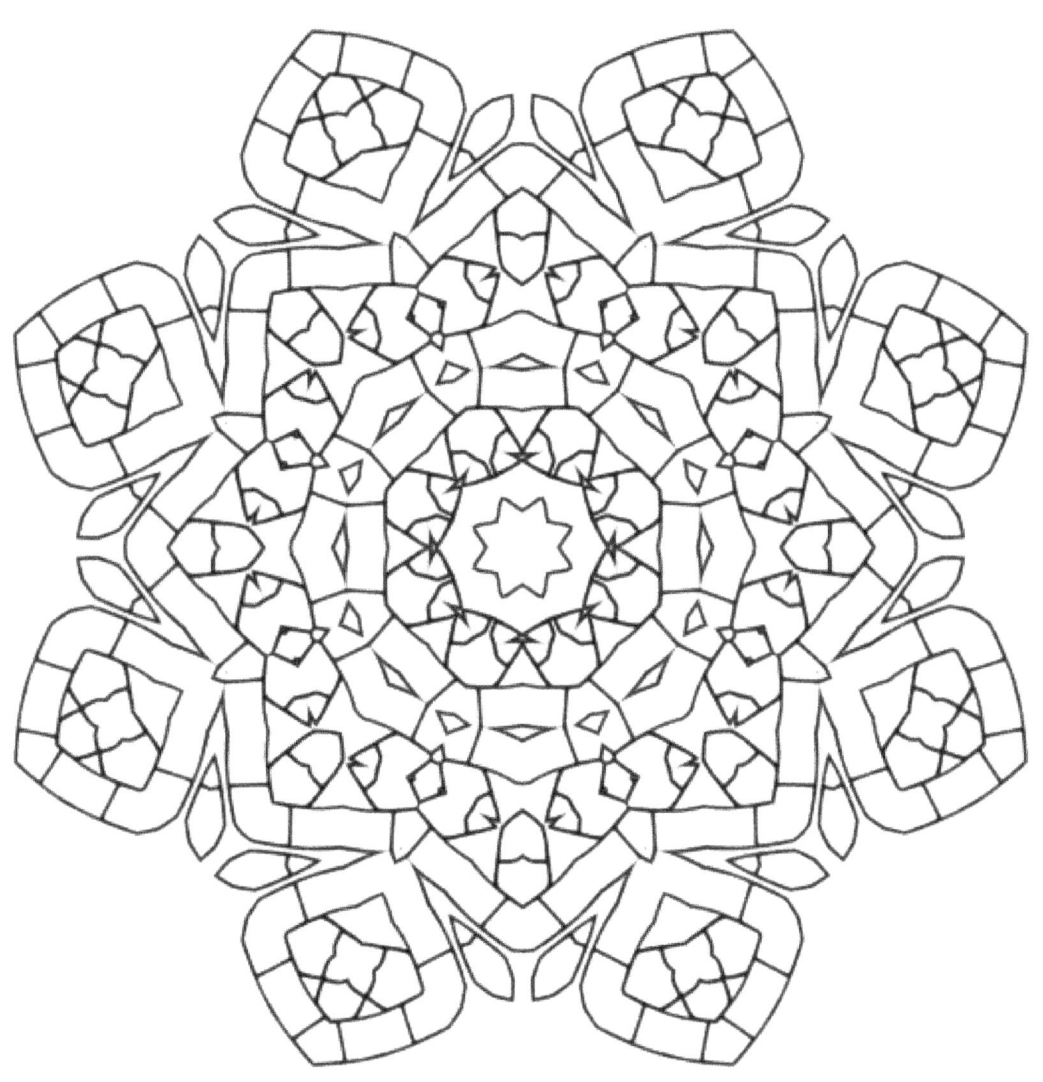

Mandala 5

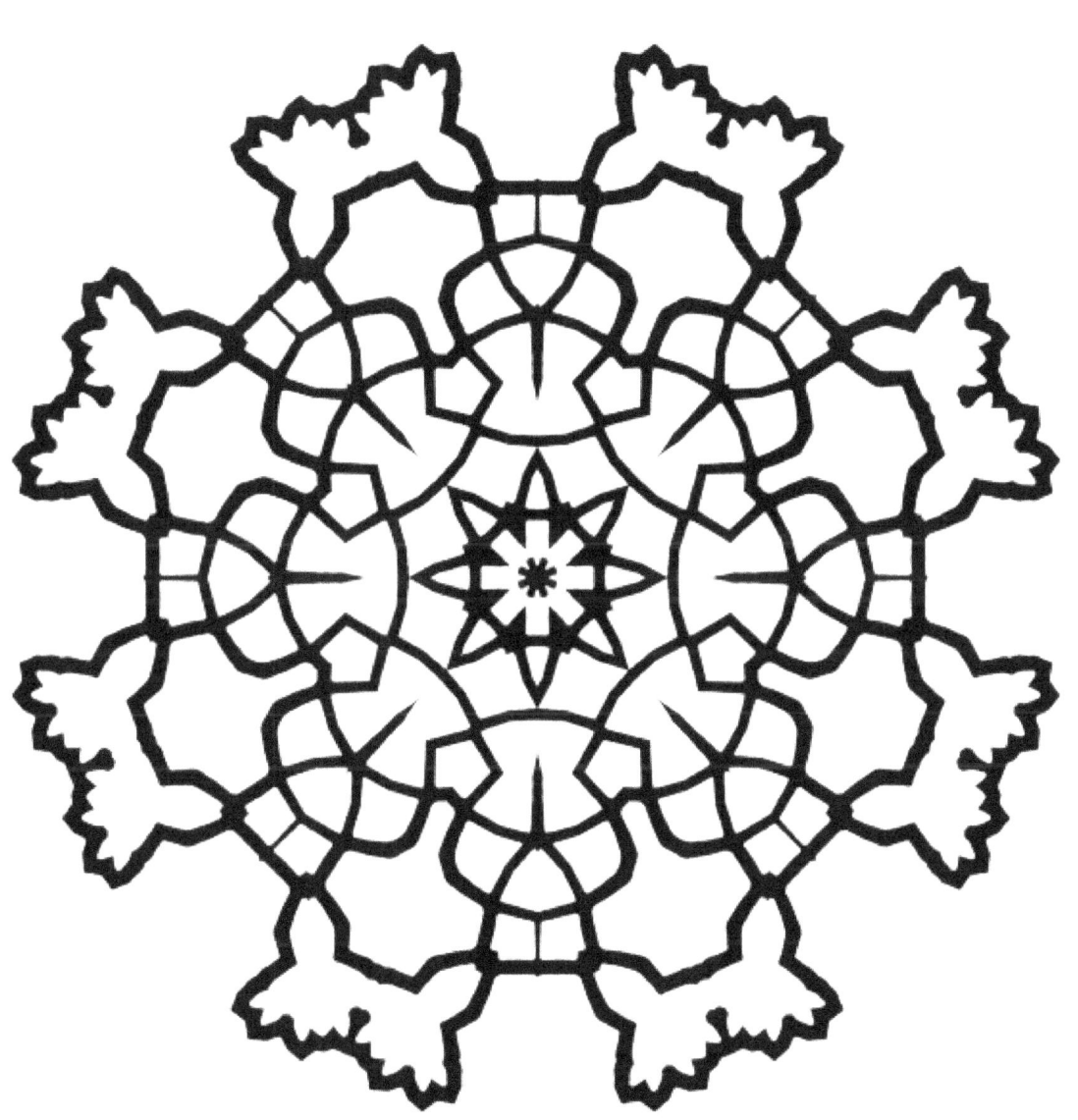

Mandala 6

Mandala 7

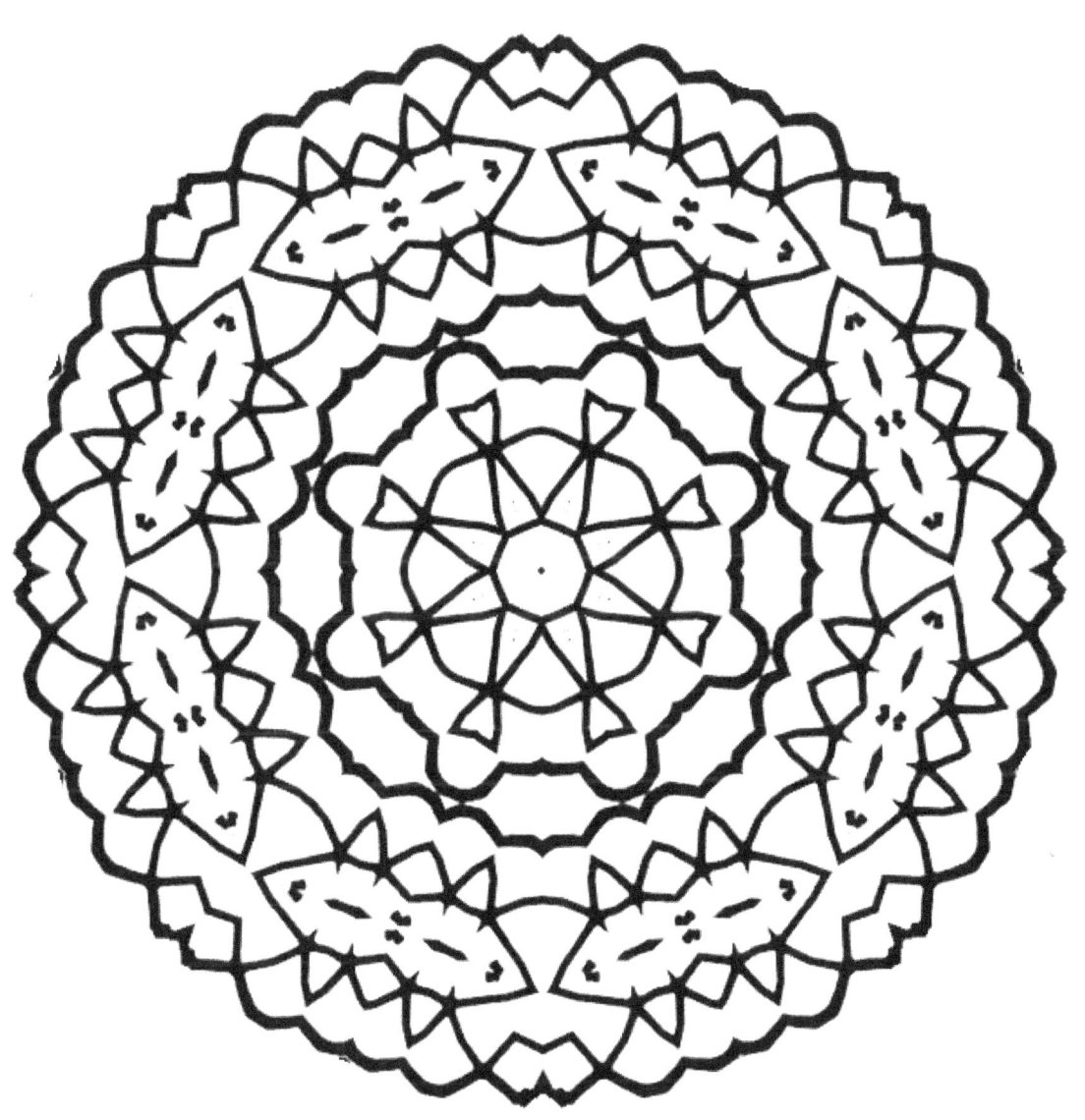

Mandala 8

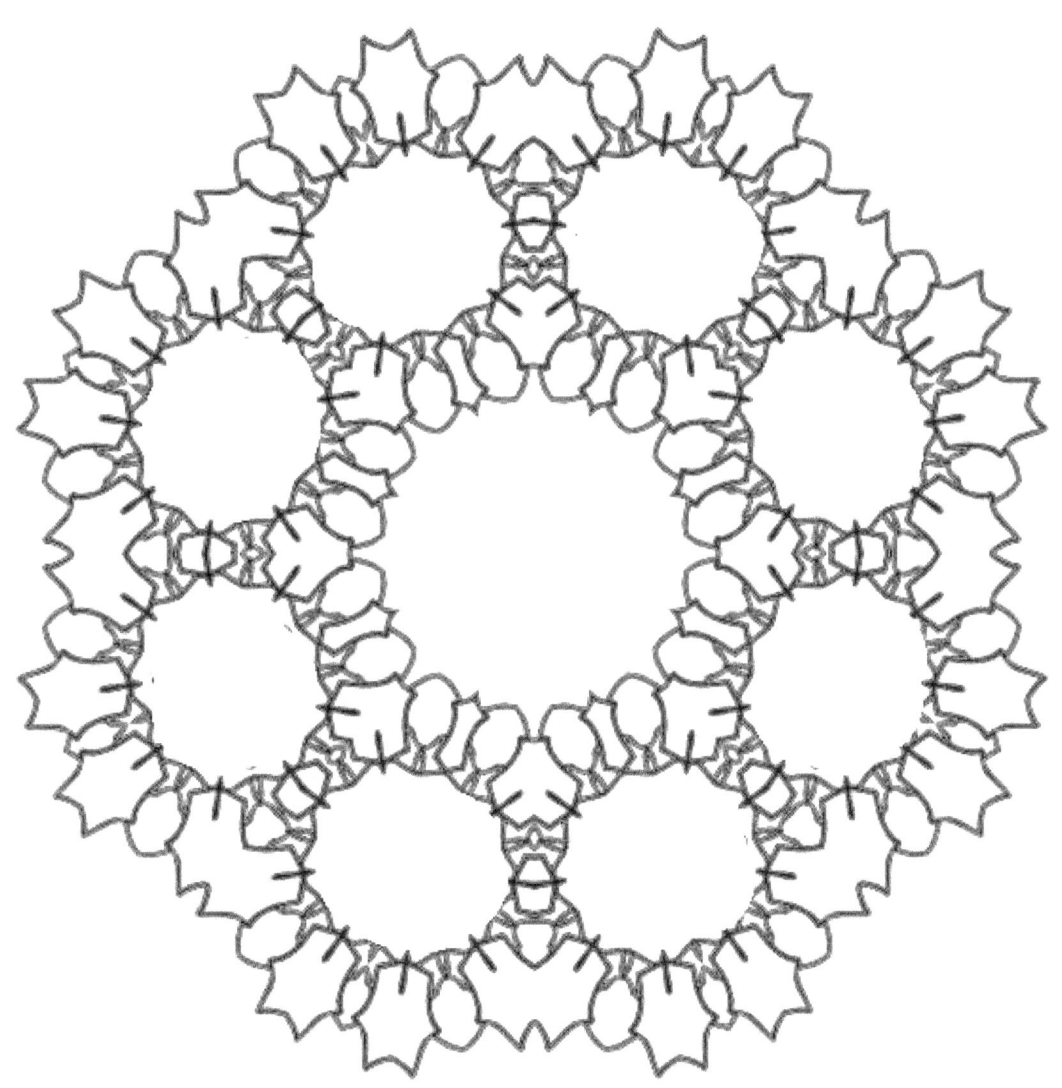

Mandala 9

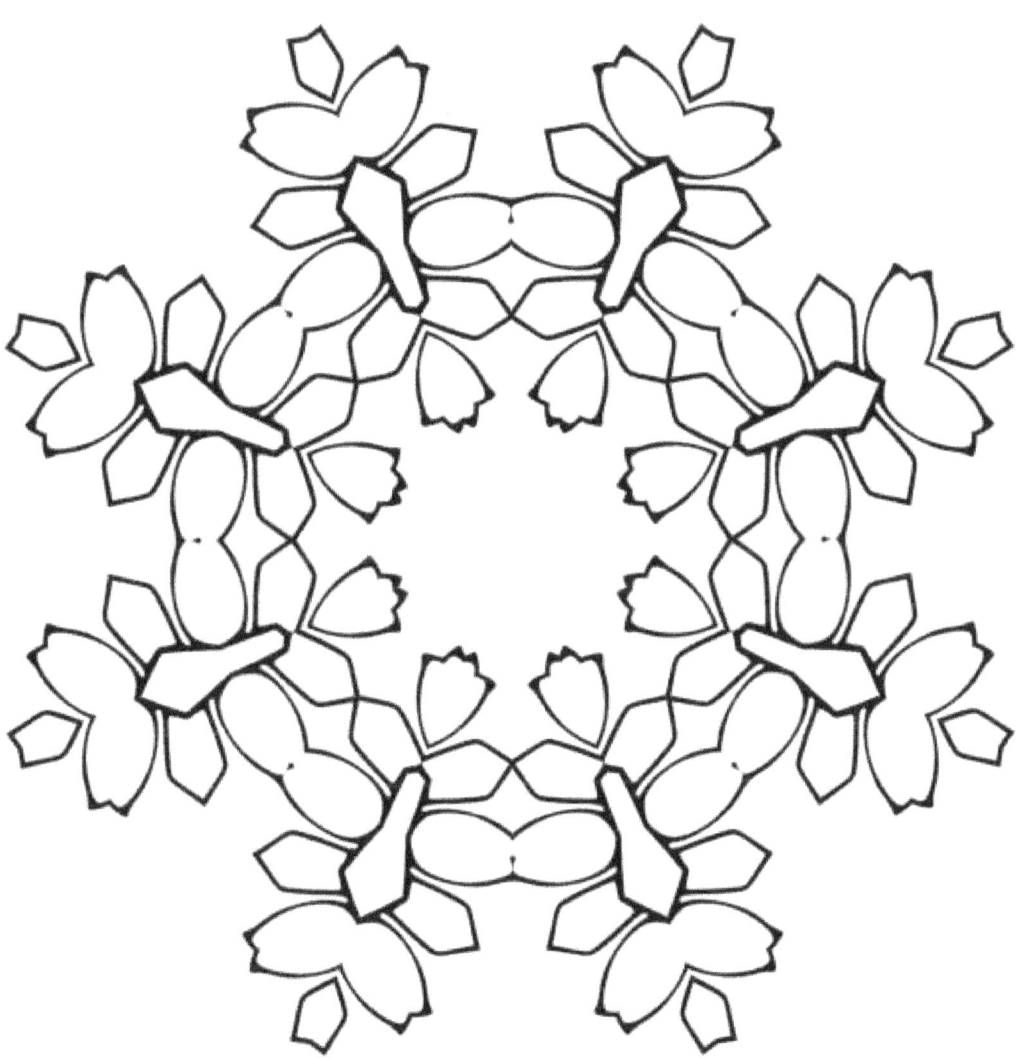

Mandala 10

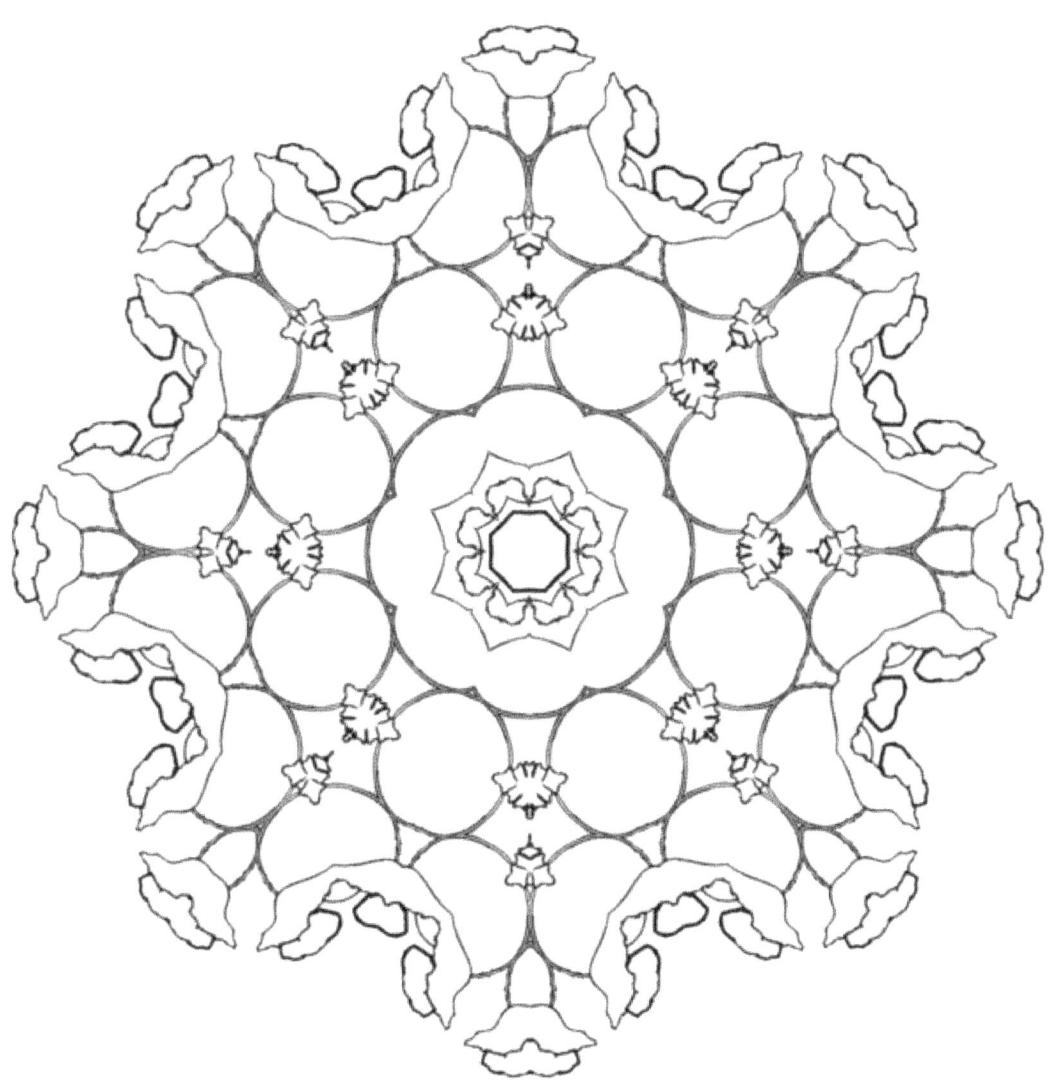

Mandala 11

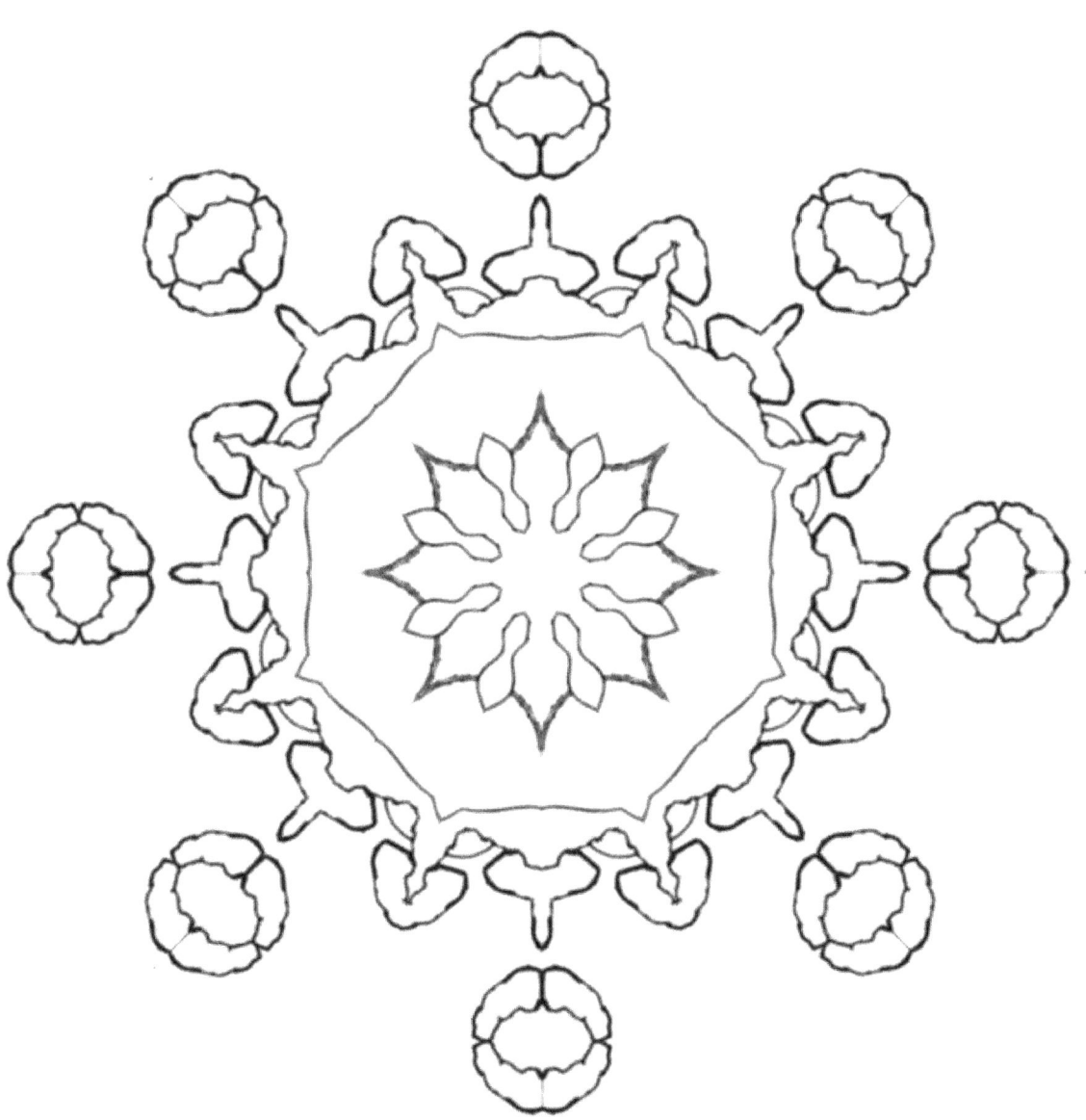

Mandala 12

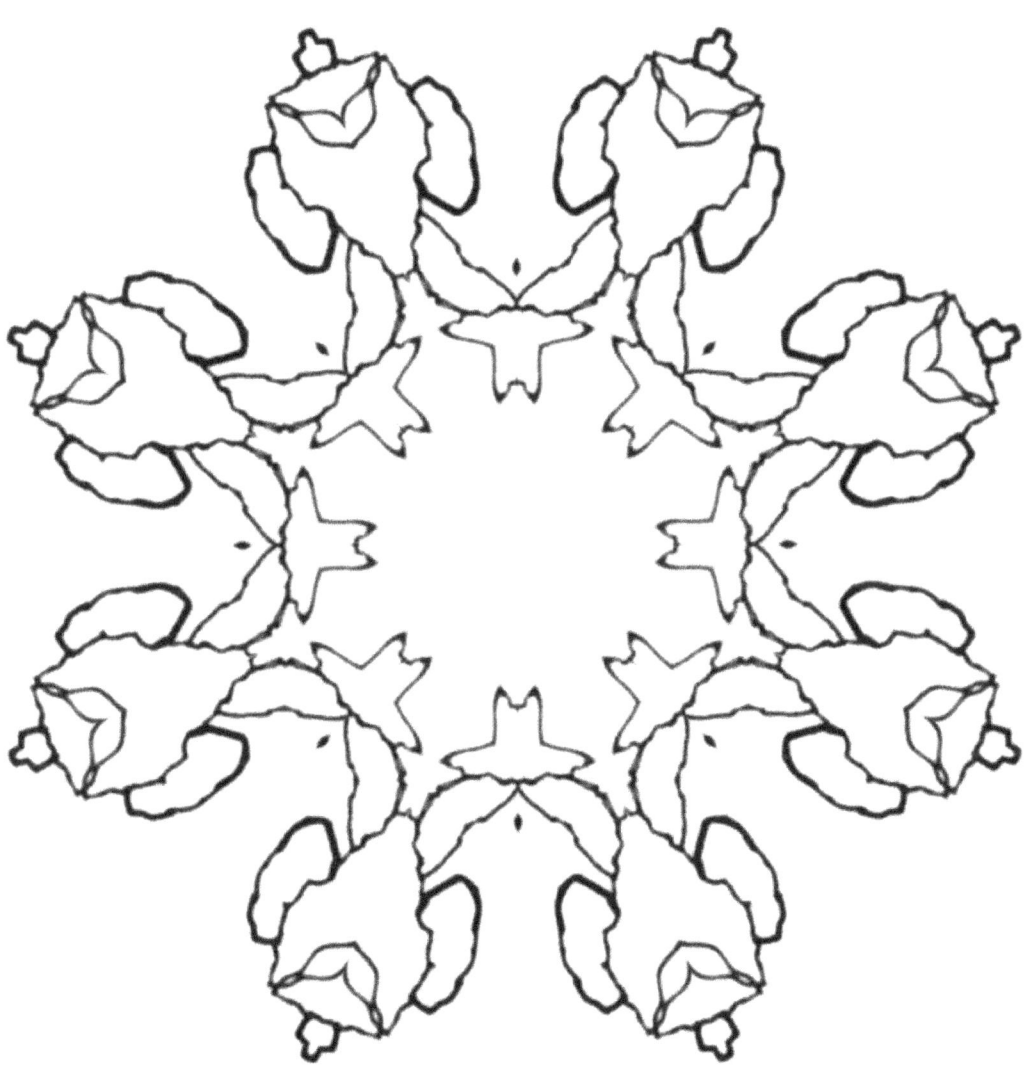

Mandala 13

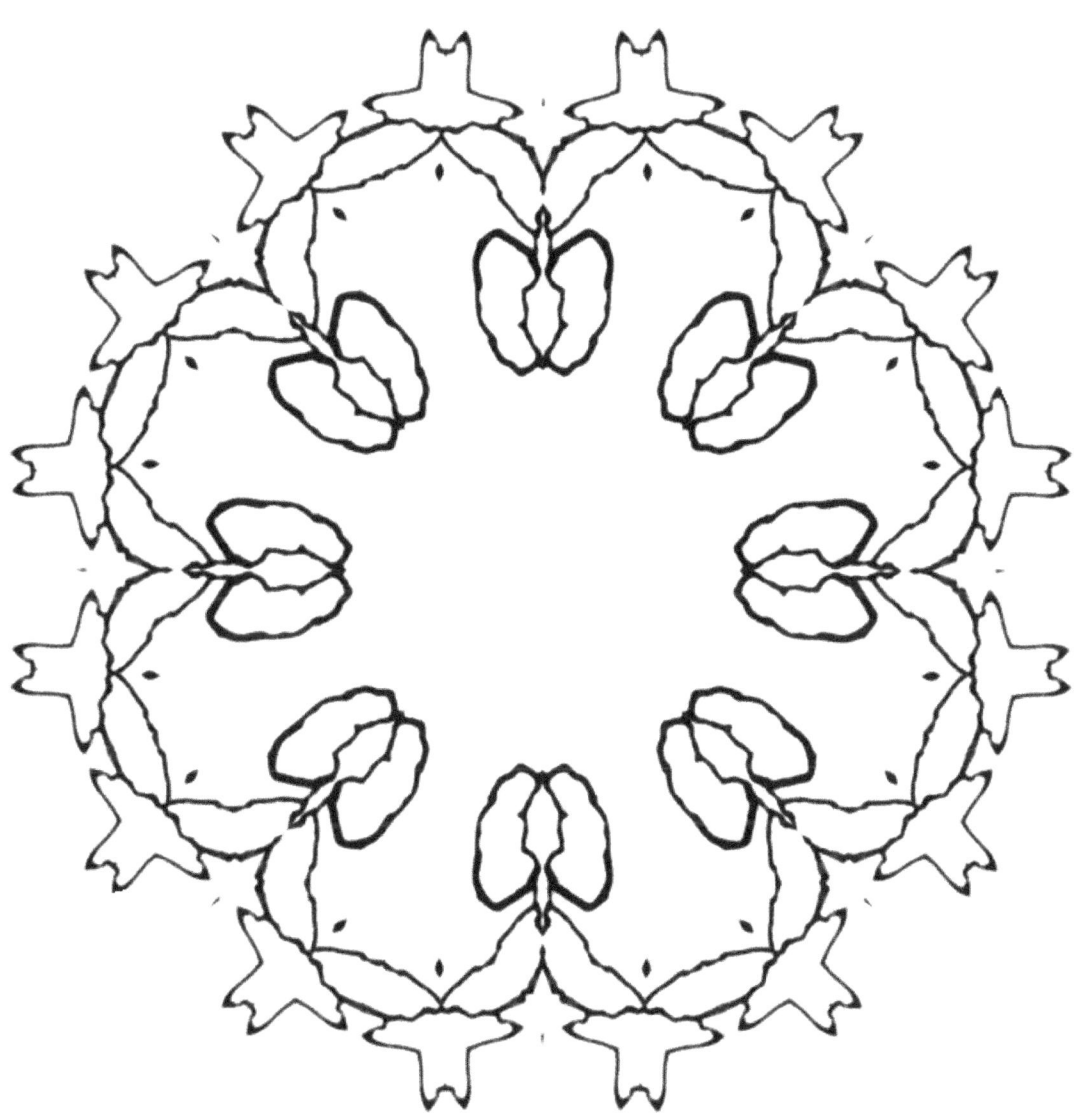

Mandala 14

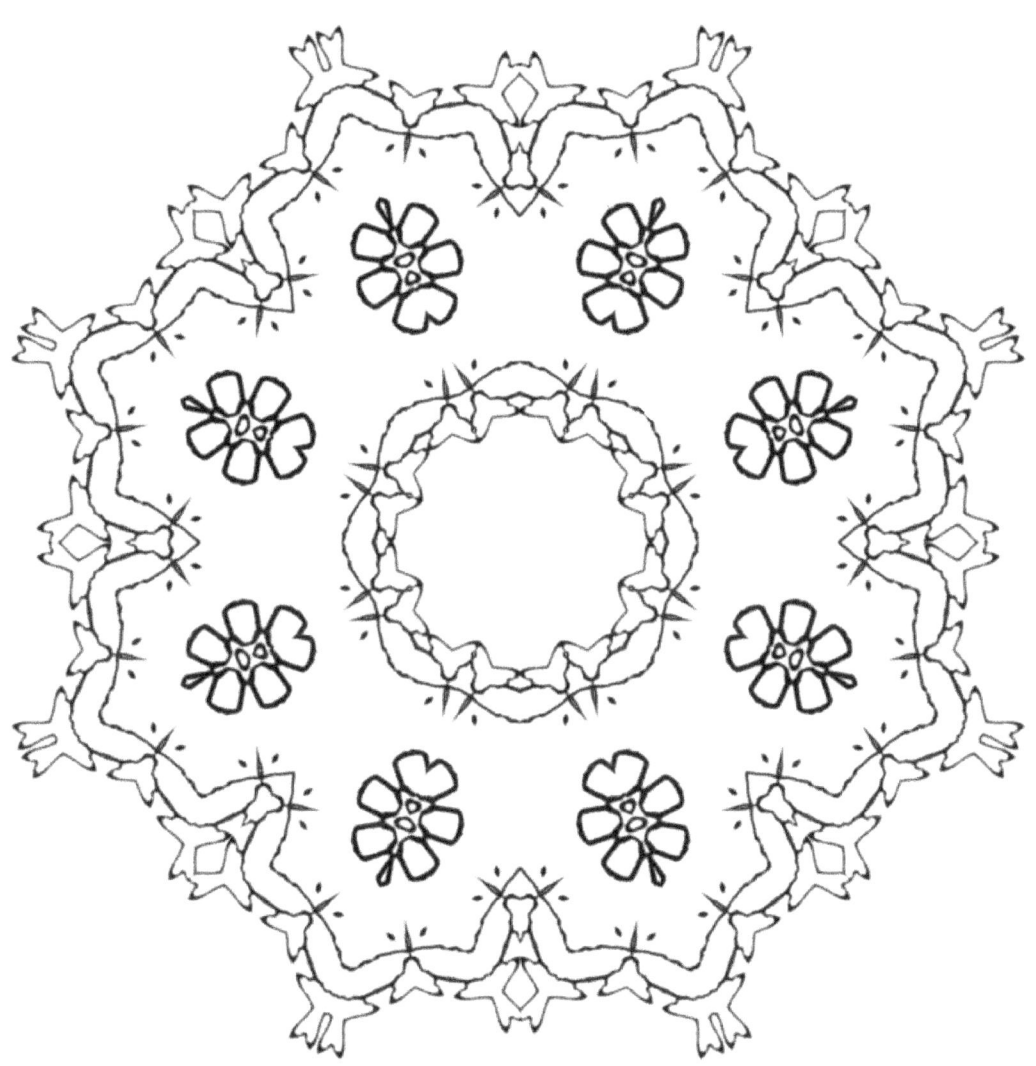

Mandala 15

Mandala 16

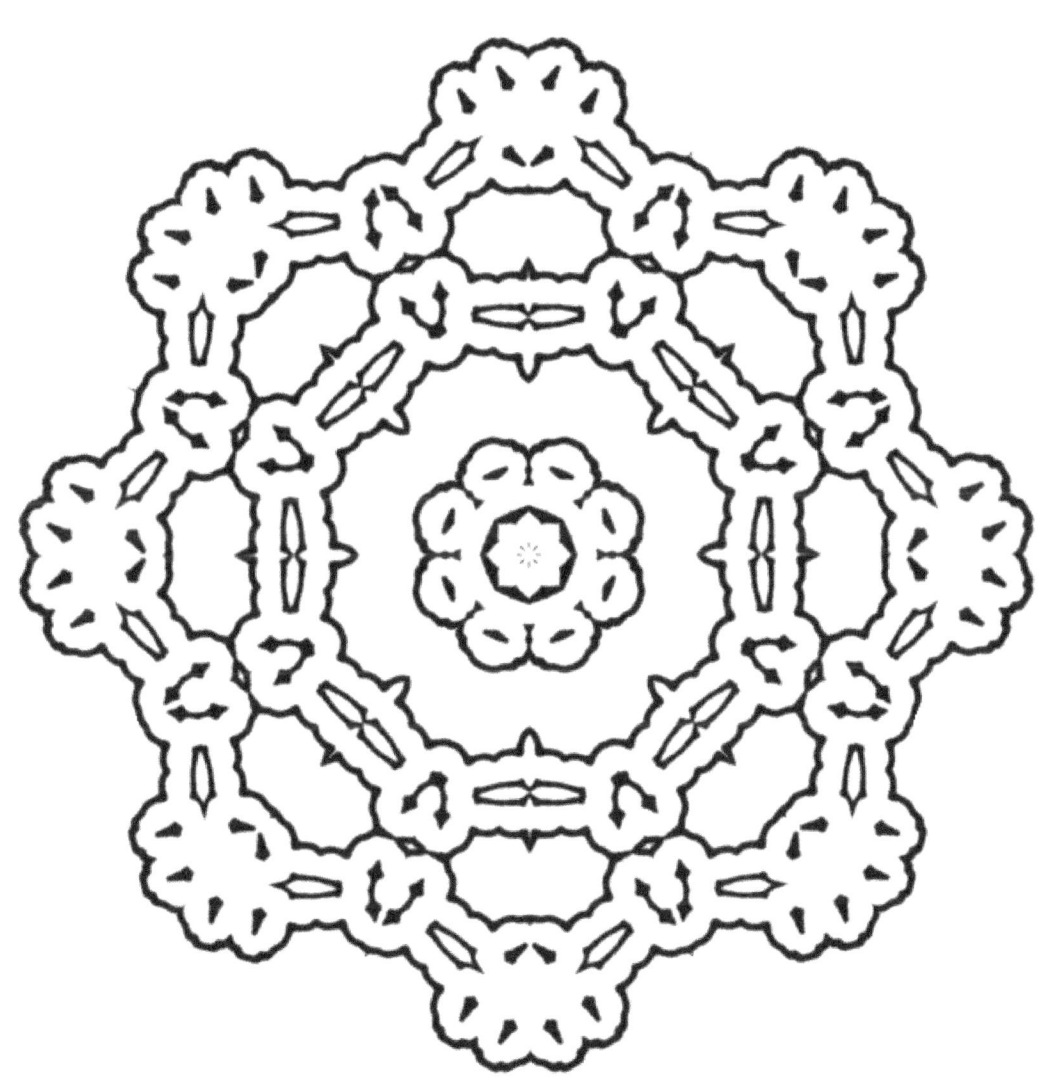

Mandala 17

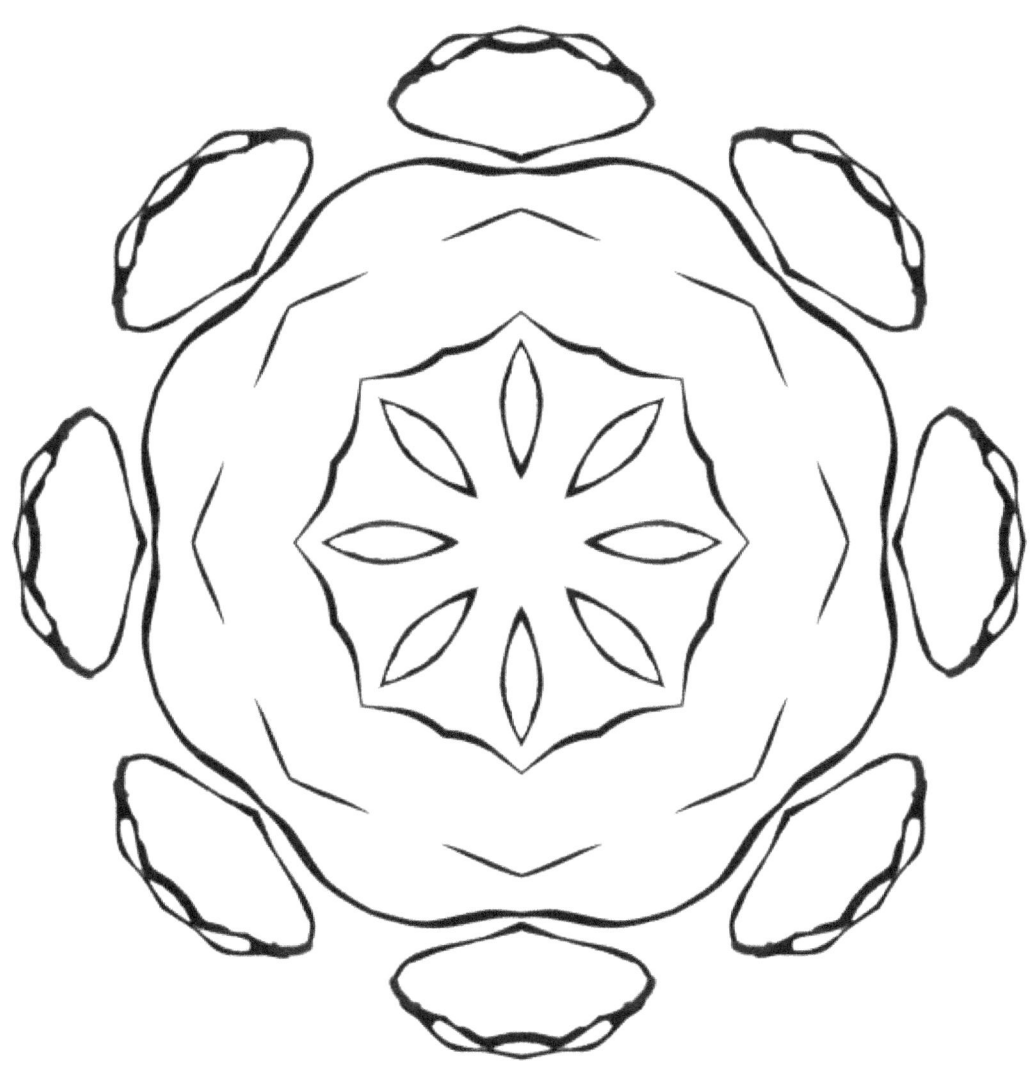

Mandala 18

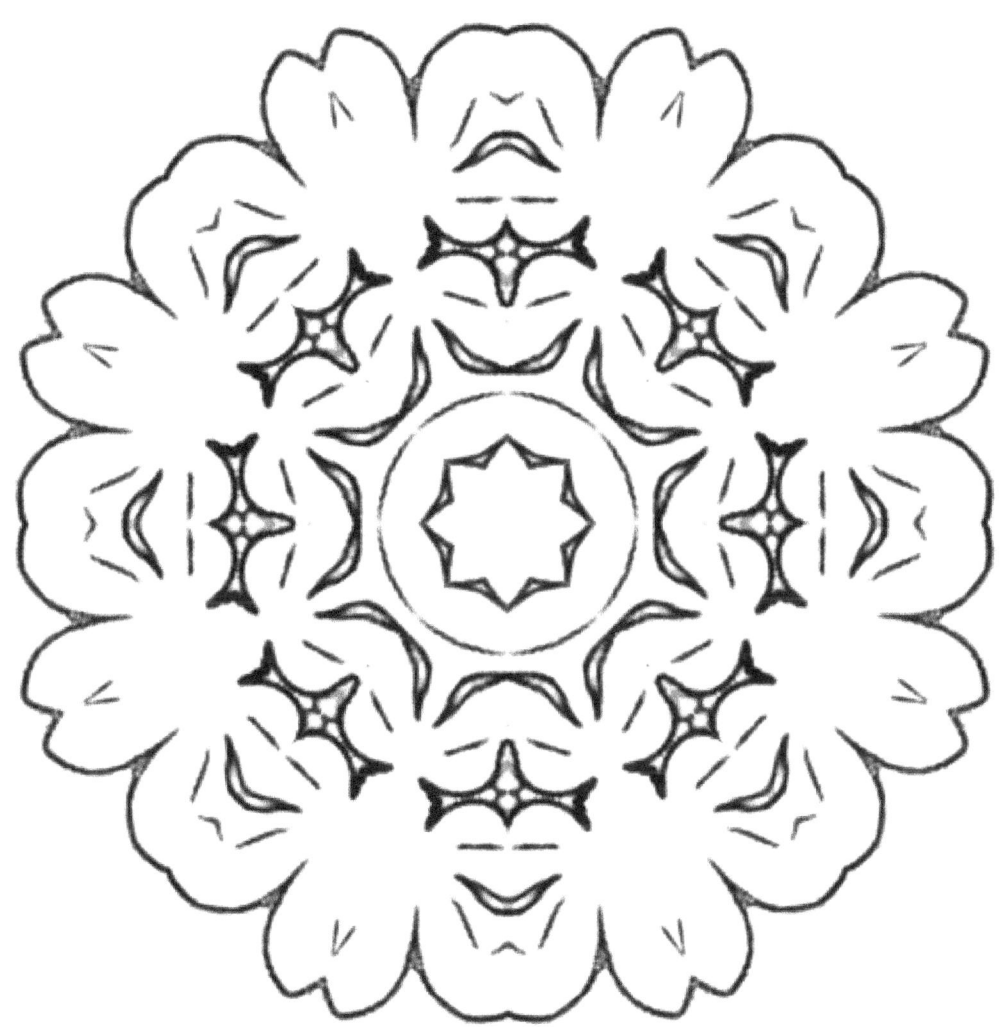

Mandala 19

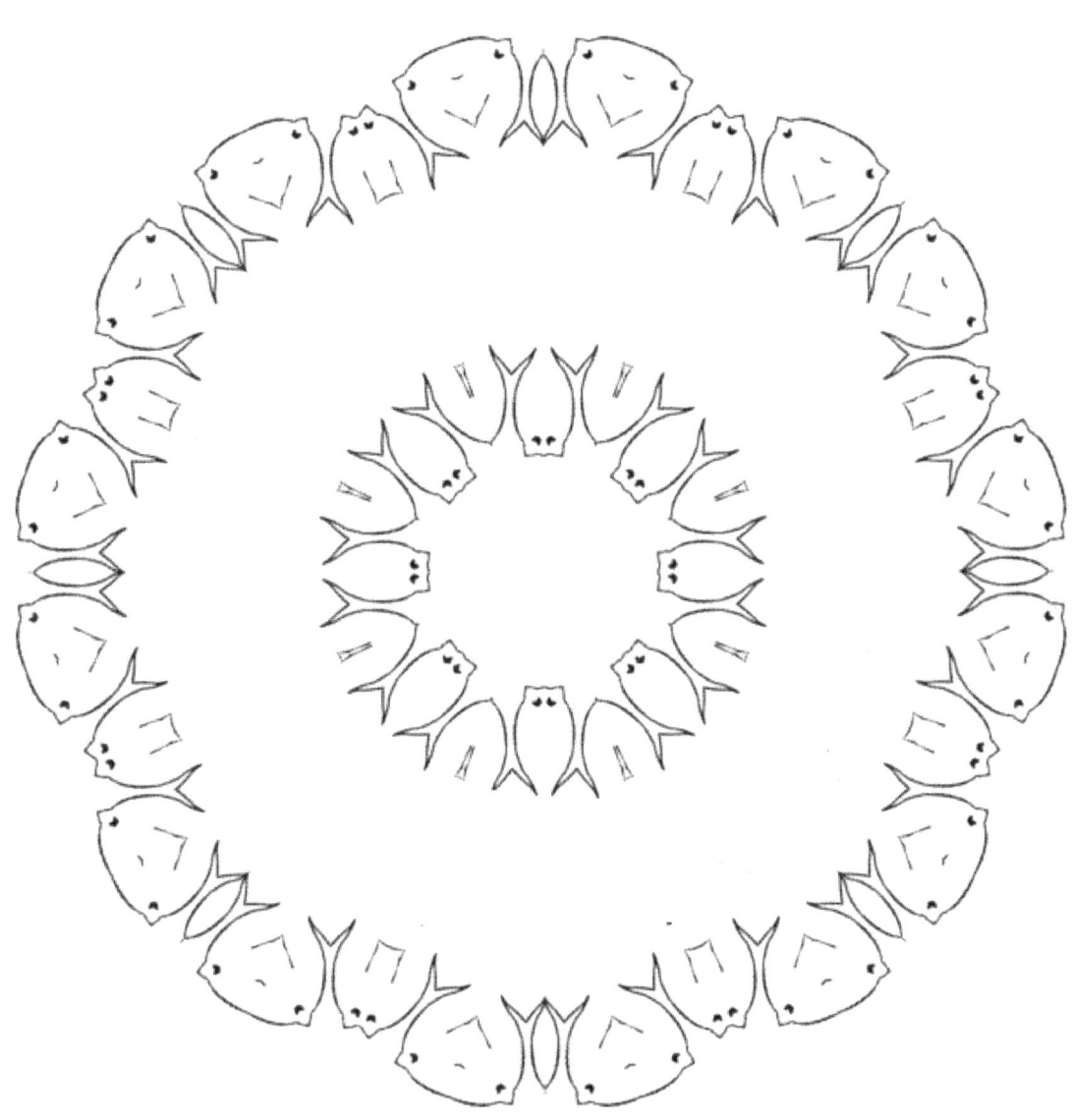

Mandala 20

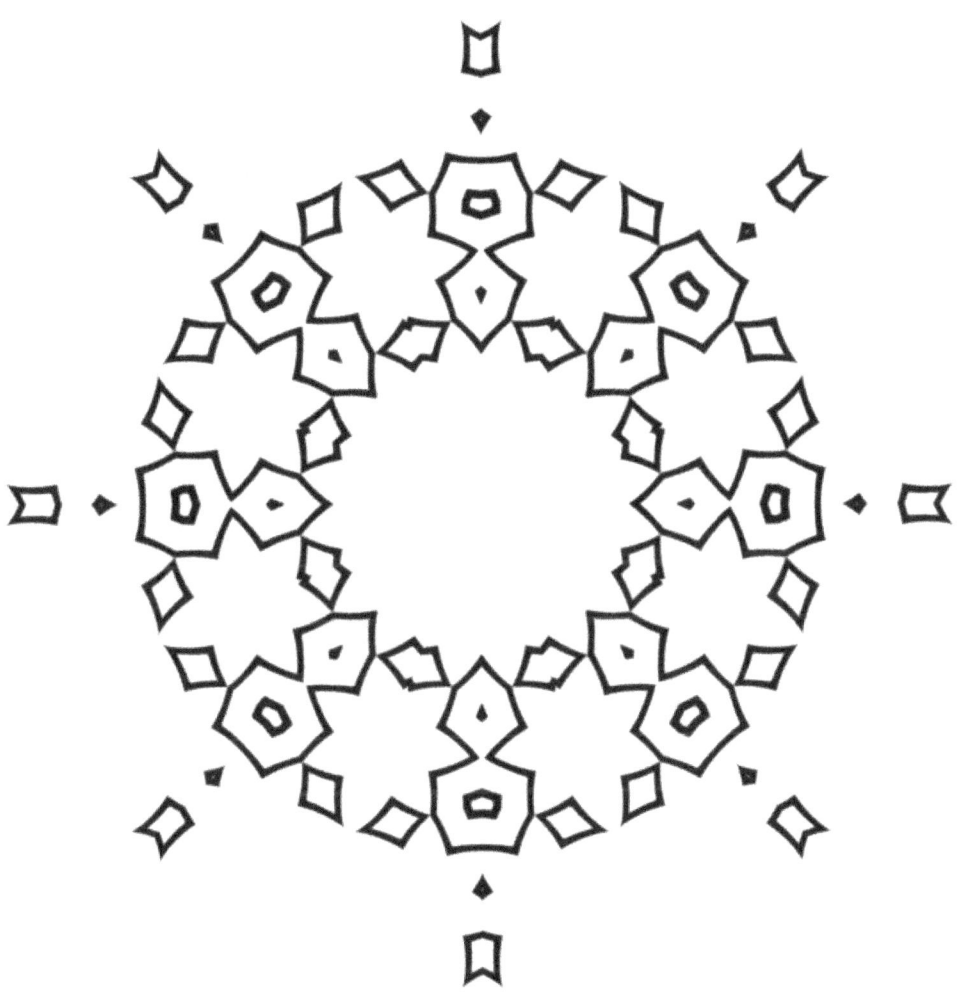

Mandala 21

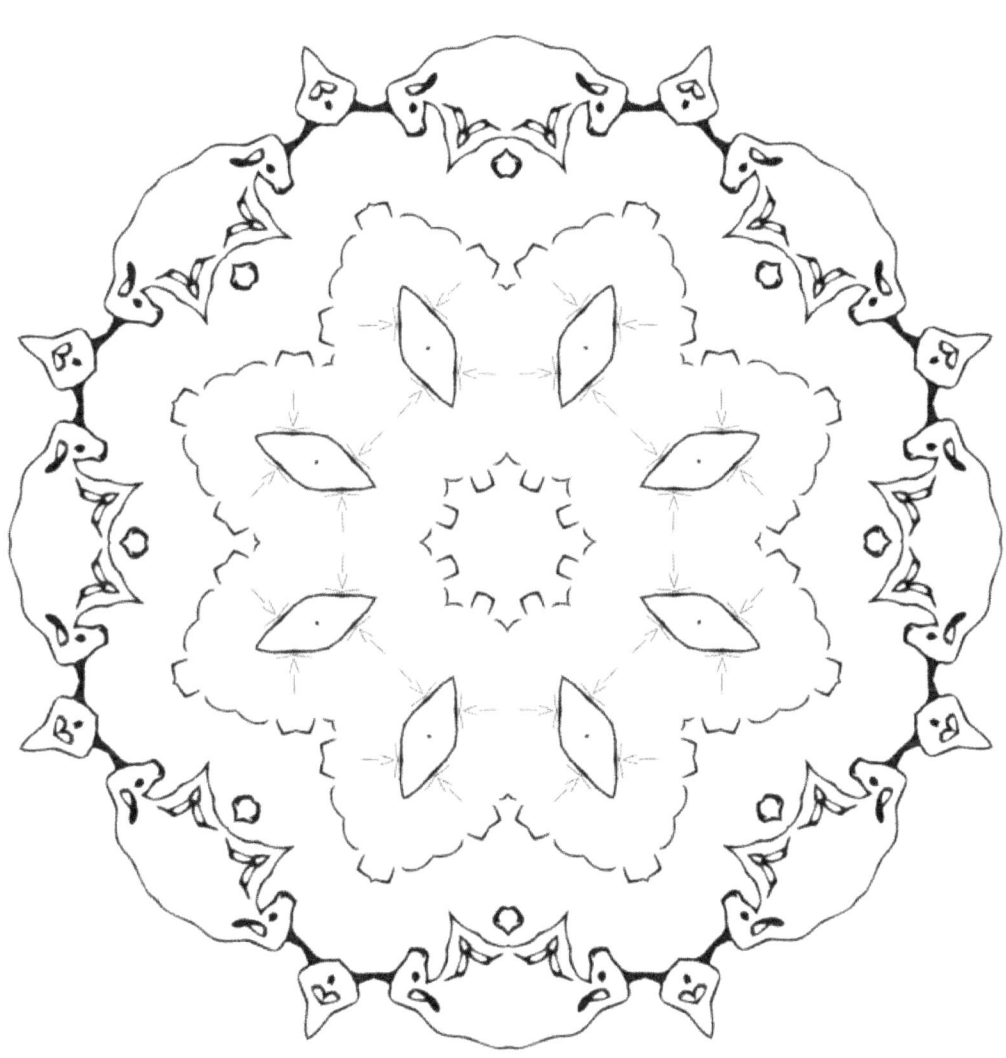

Mandala 22

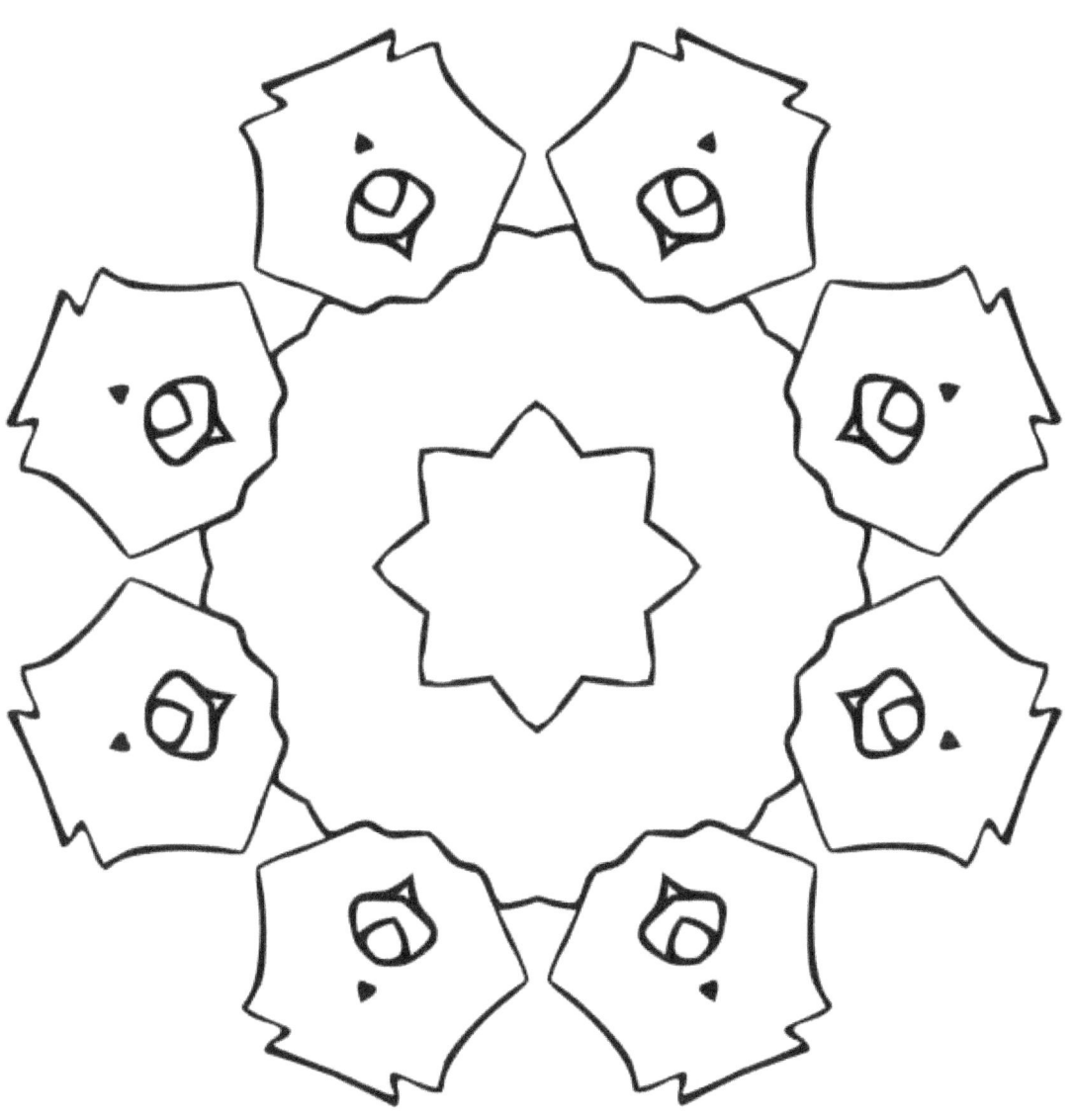

Mandala 23

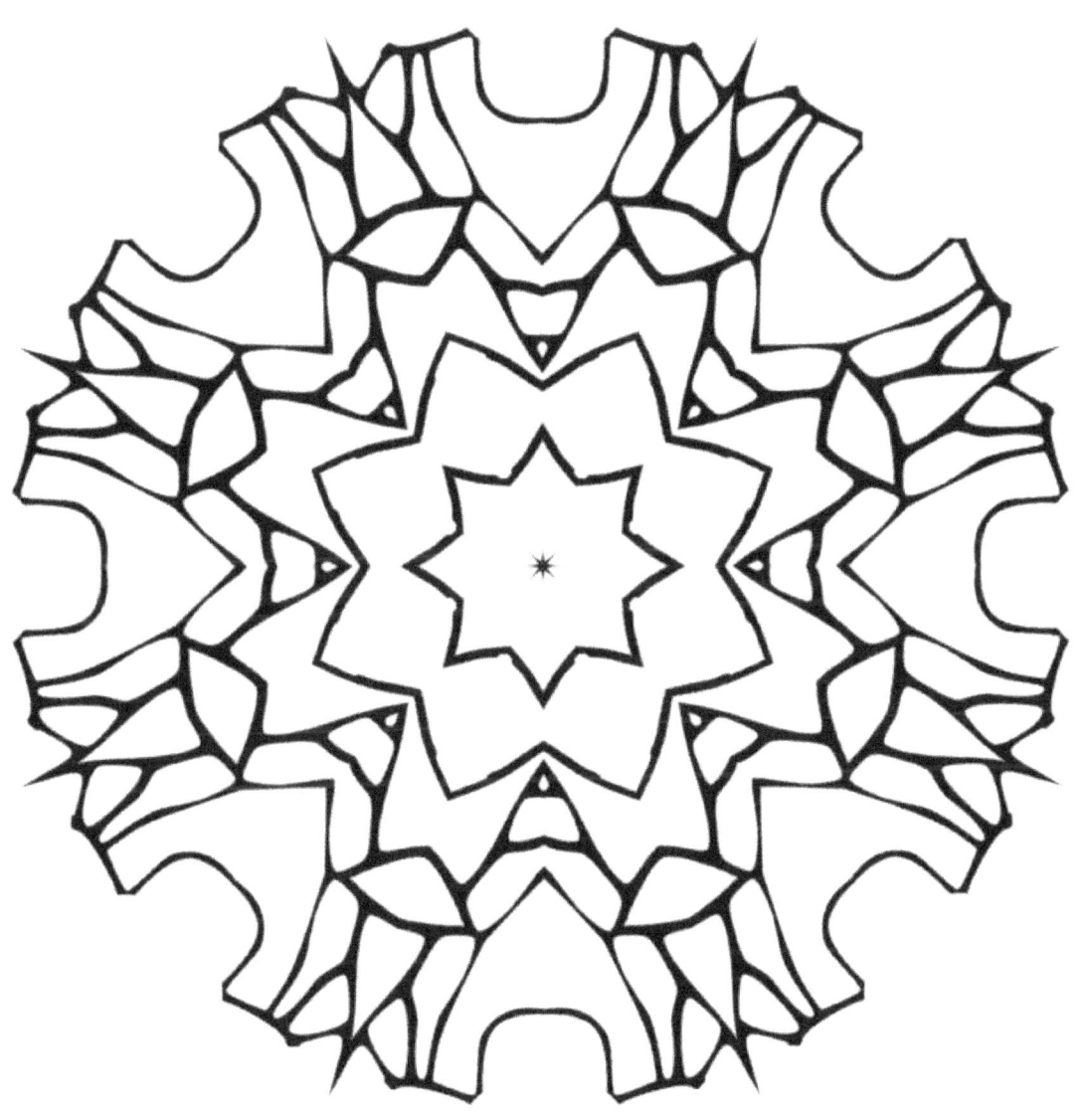

Mandala 24

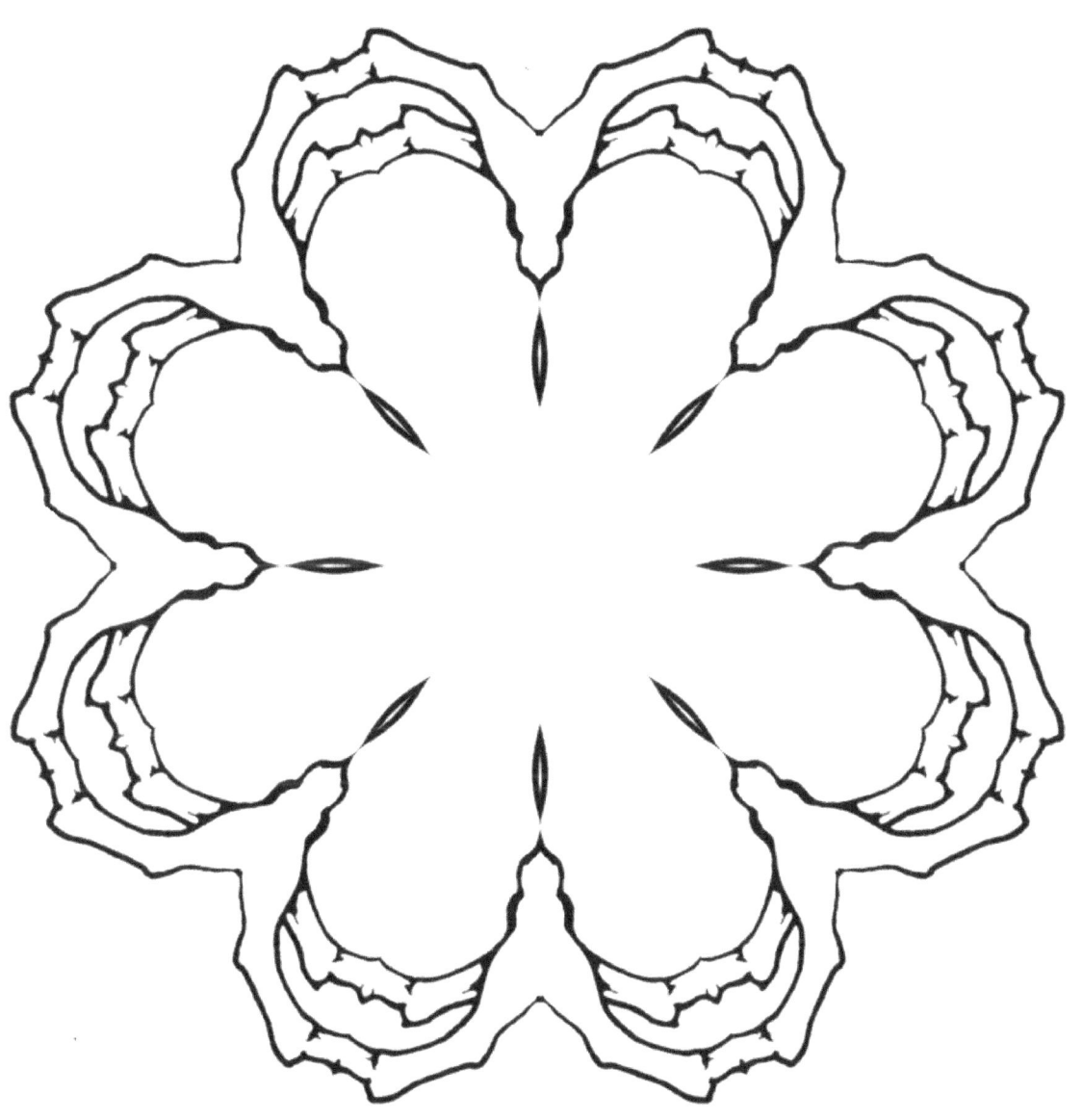

Mandala 25

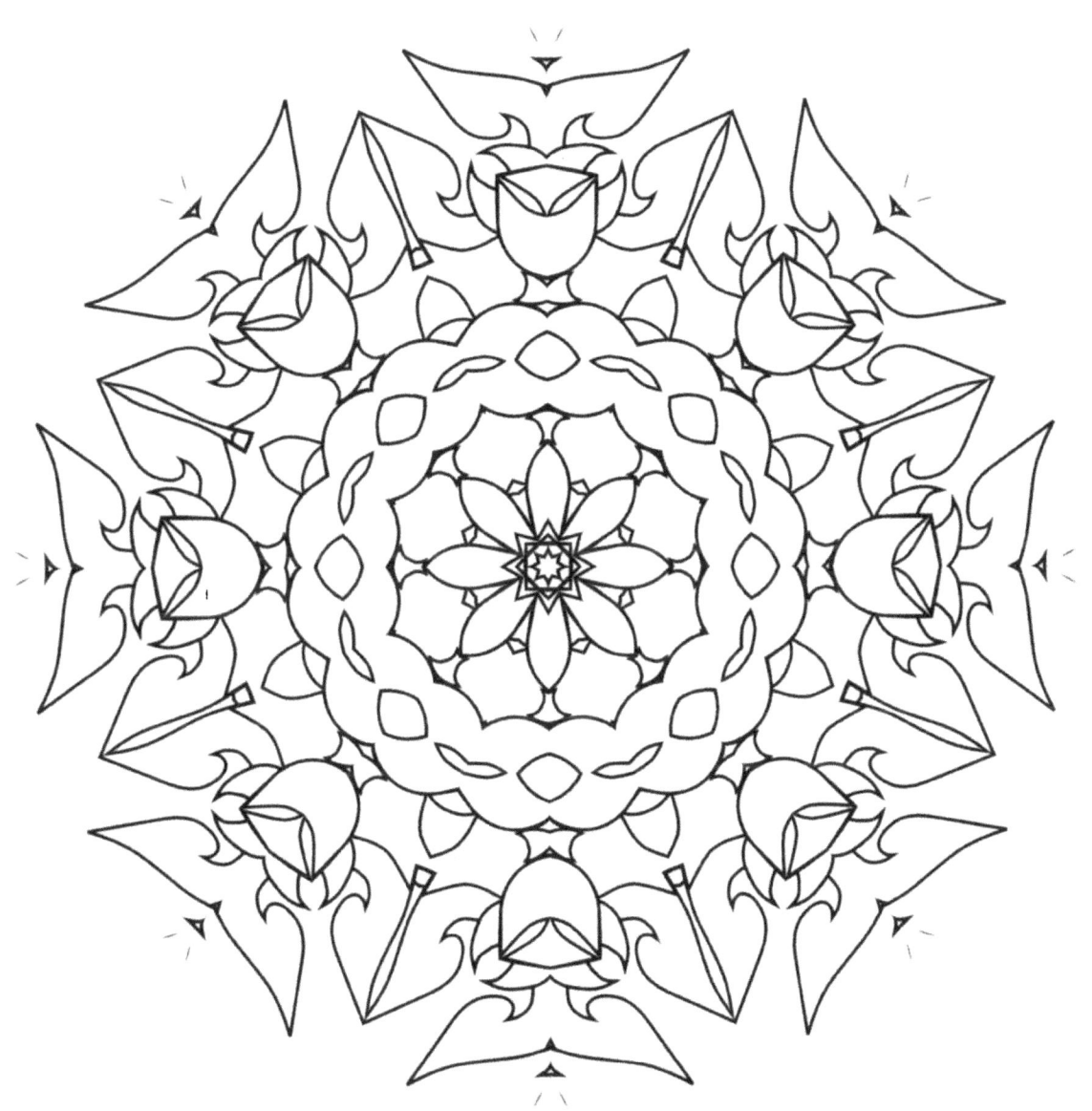

ABOUT THE AUTHOR

VIOLA HALLS IS AN ILLUSTRATOR WHO LOVE DRAWING, PAINTING AND GRAPHIC DESIGNING. NOW, SHE JUST FOUND THAT SHE LOVE DESIGNING MANDALAS AND OTHER KIND OF COLORING BOOKS. YOU CAN CONTACT HER BY **VIOLAHALLSBOOK@GMAIL.COM**

www.ingramcontent.com/pod-product-compliance
Lightning Source LLC
Chambersburg PA
CBHW080648180526
45168CB00008B/3341